THE MINORITY HOMESCHOOLER'S GUIDE

Volume 1

The Minority Homeschooler's Guide is a self-help book for minority home educators and minorities desiring more information on homeschooling.

by Johnson & Feyi Obamehinti

"Train up a child in the way he should go: and when he is old,he will not depart from it"

Proverbs 22:6

Home Education is possible for minorities and is indeed an option for all.

ACKNOWLEDGMENTS

Our foremost thanks to God, for His ever sustaining grace and wisdom in making this possible. Psalms 127 :1 sums it all up " Except the Lord builds the house, they labor in vain that buildeth" KJV

Our sincere thanks to all the wonderful families of our local support groups, through whose questions, inquires and comments brought about this book, Thanks for believing in the vision, enough to support it and stand by it.

Thanks, also to Angela Whitaker and her precious family- our Dallas group editor who has used her skills to help mold and shape many of our writings. Janice Craig, a friend and homeschool mom of nine whose life has inspired us to keep on keeping on.

Thanks, also to Kirk and Beverly McCord who

was used of God to open doors for us to share the vision of reaching out to minority home educators in their annual bookfairs- they gave wings to the vision.

Without our children's love and support, this information would only be a dream. Thanks to Lola, Layo and Lade for teaching us that homeschooling is a lifestyle not a formula you follow, but a way of life that you enjoy. Special thanks to Lola, (our oldest daughter) who came up with this appropriate title. We are blessed to have each one of you in our lives.

TABLE OF CONTENTS

INTRODUCTION

Another annual bookfair, and it was very encouraging to see faces of different families represented. From Asians, to Hispanics, to African-Americans to Native Americans and Anglos with adopted minority children. About seven years ago, one might probably see one or two minority families at the bookfair, or a homeschool event. Things have changed within the homeschool movement, God is drawing minority families in to homeschooling. Although the numbers are still low compared to the numbers of minorities in our private or public schools.

Hence this book. Through our almost ten years of homeschooling as a minority, God has used our lives to draw in, to encourage, to motivate and challenge minorities into the homeschool lifestyle.

Home schooling has become a well known alternative to public education in America. Many who would never themselves venture on this lifestyle admire and highly esteem the families that do. The character and intellectual competence of home-schooled children intrigue them.

According to the research study sponsored by the Home School Legal Defense Association (HSLDA) in 1998 and conducted by Dr. Lawrence Rudner, minorities (African Americans, Hispanics, Asians, Native Americans and Jews) comprise 6% of the homeschooling community. This compares to 32.8% in the public schools nationally. Lack of support, lack of knowledge, and fear have played a key role in the low number of minority home educators.

This book will uncover the myths of home-schooling being just for some and not for all. A glimpse of the lifestyle of homeschooling dates back to Bible days, specific commandments given in the Bible about training up children (which by the way is what home education is all about) is for all Christians willing to follow their Father's command. This book also taps into the variety that exists among minorities in this great journey of home education. This is a representation of the rainbow: different colors, yet it was the one sign of covenant that God made with humanity after the flood. (Genesis 9:13)

As a minority homeschooling family, we know first hand the struggles, and challenges that come from friends and relatives that think we have betrayed the educational system that was made for us through the public school system. Yet, we know the unspeakable joy and fulfillment that comes from obeying our heavenly father as we train our children for His glory. Not an easy task, parenting by itself is a tough job, then add a homeschool lifestyle, it is by His grace indeed.

You'll find out that homeschooling could be a means reclaiming our youth in the twenty- first century. A means of rebuilding strong families hence producing strong and effective disciples for the Lord in these last days.

Chapter 1

HOME EDUCATION AND THE BIBLE

The Bible is the blue print for all who have chosen to live life God's way. Many will like to say the Bible is just an historical book, that no longer has any bearing upon our current society. For thousands of families around the world, that have followed this "Great Book" the results have been the convincing factor that indeed the Bible is not just a historical book but the living words of an Omnipotent God to his people.

In the book of Deuteronomy, chapter 6, we find the guidelines for families in training Godly children that will glorify Him in the land whither they go to possess. Applying the context of this word to our lives today, we see the footprints of home education. *Verses 7-9 says "And thou shalt teach them diligently unto thy children and shalt talk of them when thou sittest in thine house, and when thou walkest by the way, and when thou liest down, and when thou risest up. And thou shalt bind them for a sign upon thine hand, and they shall be as frontlets between thine eyes. And thou shalt write them upon the posts of thy house and on thy gates."*

Home Education is the direct teaching of one's child(ren) at home by the parents. This teaching comprises of godly character and academics. When the Bible talks about "and thou shalt teach them diligently unto thy children" it refers to the laws God passed on to the children of Israel through his servant Moses. So, God is saying teach them my laws, my commandments, how to love me, how to serve me, how to worship me, how to honor me, how to live for me etc. The parent is the one who receives this responsibility, for the word says "and thou shalt teach them diligently unto *thy children*". This is referring to home education, it is a direct teaching of certain principles by the parent to the child.

These certain principles to be taught is so vital that they have to be talked about even when relaxing (when thou sittest in thine house). The word *house* is indicative of where the majority of these teaching must take place. The latter verse says to "write them upon the posts of thy house and on thy gates".

The word house is mentioned again. Repetition of words in the Bible is not a waste, but signifies emphasis. Home education takes diligence which according to II Peter 1: 5 is a process which when attained secures productivity and effectiveness in the life of a Christian. Deuteronomy 6: 7 talks about "how" to teach these certain principles to our children. It says to teach them *diligently.* This means consistently working hard to achieve a goal, in this regards, the goal is to teach those certain principles to our children until they begin to do those things naturally without any prompt or help. The principles of worshipping God, loving God, honoring Him, is taught until these things become second nature in their lives.

Many will like to say home education is a new movement that surfaced, about 25 years ago, but the truth of the matter is, its been around since Bible days. These principles were taught in the house, by parents whose main desire was to pass on their faith to their children, so that each generation knew the God of Abraham, Isaac and Jacob. It was the parents acceptance of this great commission that preserved the faith through each generation. To ensure a Godly society, God gave a commandment, using the vehicle of home education. It had to be done at home on a consistent basis and the results were assured in that the children will desire to keep the commandments of the Lord, His testimonies, and statutes with all their heart-verse 17.

Looking at diverse cultures around the world, we find that imparting family principles is very important. For example the Jewish culture, parents teach the children how to honor God. Hannah did this for Samuel, who lived in the temple with Eli the Priest. For Samuel to appreciate the God of his mother, who answered her prayer in opening her womb, Samuel had to be taught about that God. In the Yoruba - African culture, parents teach their children how to farm by taking the children daily to the farm. Home education affords parents to "pass on" their faith to their children.

Apprenticeship has gained ground in the last 5 years, the above description is what apprenticeship is all about. Home education is as old as the records in biblical days, what has happened over the years is a refining of the art of home education. There are many pointers in the Bible to home education, this helps to validate the current movement of home education in America and around the world.

A radio announcer once gave the acronym of the Bible as:

Basic
Instruction
Before
Leaving
Earth

The basic instructional manual for us as Christians is the Bible, it covers all we need to know about home education. If we have chosen to follow this way of life, then answering to our critics about the validity of home education is really something that can not be understood by them. We will like to think that following the biblical principles(parents teaching their children principles that are vital to life) has so much to do with the great results we see today in the homeschooling community.

One might ask the question-what would Jesus think of homeschoolers if he was present in our day today. He wouldn't be shocked at all. It wasn't called "homeschooling" in Jesus's day, but the principle of parents taking charge of their child's education or learning has been in existence since the beginning of time, when children were born into families. Jesus himself was "homeschooled" by his earthly father, Joseph. The Bible records that he helped with the carpentry business. One thing was definite as Jesus advanced in His earthly ministry, he taught the Master's Principle. What does that mean?

Mark 10: 43-44 shows us clearly what that is. "Whoever wishes to become great among you shall be your servant; and whoever wishes to be first among you shall be slave of all". Although Jesus was not a revolutionary in the political sense, many of His teachings were startling and revolutionary, and none more than those on leadership. In the contemporary world, the term servant has a lowly connotation, but that was not so as Jesus used it. Indeed, He elevated it, equating it with greatness, and that was certainly a revolutionary concept. Most of us would have no objection to being masters, but servant-hood holds little attraction. The Bible verse above, demonstrates a sharp contrast to the world's idea of who a leader is.

So, how does this relate to homeschooling? Dad, takes the role of a servant when he leads his family in fulfilling the conviction of homeschooling. He gladly provides for his family. Mom, on the other hand takes the role of a servant when she accepts this noble challenge to nurture the children and serve her family. The world's view of success is different from this. The children also learn from their "role models/parents" what leadership is all about according to the Master's Principle. Their idea of leadership is formed by watching and imitating their leaders (parents). Instilling politeness, respect, meekness, gentleness, self-control, reverence for God and authority, patience and contentment in our children is following the master's principle, for it takes all the above virtues and much more to indeed be a godly leader for His glory.

Chapter 2

WHAT IS HOMESCHOOLING?

Homeschooling has become a well-known alternative to public education in America. Many who would never themselves venture into this lifestyle admire and highly esteem the families that do. The character and intellectual competence of homeschooled children intrigue them. Homeschooling dates back to biblical times in which specific commandments were given for training and nurturing children. Homeschooling is a "lifestyle" in which parents assume all responsibilities for educating their children spiritually, socially and academically.

Some choose to take on all aspects of training and educating while others chose to delegate some of those responsibilities to others that are specially trained as their children prepare for college and adulthood. Some utilize mentorship and apprenticeship to provide a well-rounded education for their children. In the state of Texas where we reside, homeschooling is classified as a private school, and private schools in Texas are not regulated. This allows parents adequate freedom to direct the education of their children Home educators take their parenting responsibilities very seriously. Contrary to the myth that homeschoolers are isolated, many, if not all, homeschoolers are extremely busy families. They are involved in church activities, community activities (such as sports teams), and enrichment activities (such as Scouts, 4-H Clubs, choir, music, dance).

Many of the volunteers you may see at your local libraries, hospitals, zoos, or shelters are often homeschoolers. Through the excellent network programs that exist within the home-schooling community at large, homeschoolers have the advantage of networking, and building meaningful and strong relationships. Homeschoolers use the world at large to obtain their curriculum and educational resources. Through many organized bookfairs offered throughout the year, homeschoolers have the opportunity to stock up on all their educational needs.

The increase in the number of homeschoolers in the last five years suggests that parents want more for their children and desire to provide the environment for an enriching and satisfying learning experience.

HOW DO YOU BEGIN HOME-SCHOOLING?

Just like any other major decision in your life: just start. Some pointers as you begin: Come up with a name for your homeschool (for example- The Doe's Academy). This will help as you organize how and when you'll keep your records. Decide what calendar you'll follow. Some families choose to follow their school district's calendar, so that they have the same holidays as the schools. Some families decide to use the school district calendar as a guide, in making up their own school year. They go on a six- week on and two weeks off schedule, or nine-week on and three week off rotation. Some families go year round instead, taking breaks as they see fit for vacations and rest. Remember, plan according to your family's circumstances, there is no set formula. In states where homeschool families have to register with their school district, their options are limited, since they have to follow the school calendar. Finding out what your state laws are on homeschooling is vital to your success. In chapter seven we give an insight on homeschool legislation and provide you with an appendix of the homeschool laws here in America. (From HSLDA)

WHAT SHOULD YOU TEACH?

About anything can be a course in homeschooling. You should consider the five basics as a foundation for learning: Mathematics, Grammar, Reading,

History and Spelling. Focusing on these basics for the elementary years could be beneficial in establishing a strong academic foundation. You may add to these basics based on your family's goals, interests and philosophy. In our family, Bible and Character building are part of our basic foundational curriculum for the elementary years, since our family's philosophy is living a glorifying life to God here on earth and for eternity.

The middle and high school years entails a more vigorous approach based on your child's future plans. If your child is planning for college, then the curriculum in the high school years will be mapped to meet the needs of that college or the major your child intends to pursue in college.

HOW ABOUT KEEPING RECORDS AND GRADUATION?

Some states require record keeping and some don't. If you're in a state that requires record keeping check with your state education agency on the format that is needed and follow that. For families that live in states that do not require record keeping, you have an option to keep or not to keep. We found out through many of the families we've met, that many keep records, even in states where they are not required to keep records. Some say, the odds are against you as a minority family not to keep any form of records,(relatives want to see and know what you're doing) so to protect themselves they choose to keep some form of records. Whatever form of record keeping you decide to follow, remember it takes organization and planning. You may subscribe to a record keeping service or umbrella program to keep all your records.

Graduation can be a special family affair or you may use a support group graduation ceremony. Many of the regional support groups in the nation organize annual graduation programs for homeschool families. For a certain fee, your child gets a cap and gown, refreshments, and a table to showcase his/her accomplishments (spiritually, academically, and all other extracurricular achievements). As the parent, you get to confer the diploma on your child-very emotional time for parents, as they reflect on their homeschool journey.

This all sounds great to any homeschool family. What about skeptical friends, neighbors and relatives that think you've lost your mind because you've chosen to homeschool? There is really not much you can do about that. Like anything you embark upon in life, some will believe in you to support you and some will not no matter what you do or say. So, you'll have to make up your mind that homeschooling is indeed for you. From the many testimonials we have on minority home educators, friends, neighbors and relatives do come around after years of observing the results of homeschooling. They admire the poise of your children, their blossom, their thirst for the things of God, or even their academic abilities that surpasses that of their peers. We've been asked many times by well meaning people this question "Why would any want to homeschool their children?" For us we homeschool for the following reasons:

- We have a conviction from God, a mandate to nurture our children
- We are striving to be good stewards of what has been entrusted to us—our children
- We have a glimpse of the divine purpose for the world—the family
- We are seeking for ways to be a solution rather than a problem
- We desire to be the role models for our children and not sports figures or Hollywood celebrities.

Homeschooling is a lifestyle that fits your own family situation. It's not a formula. Pursuing your family's goals is the key to your success in homeschooling. Just because another family chooses to pursue their homeschool program in a different way does not mean they are off and your family is right on target. The great enigma of homeschooling is the diversity in methods, approaches and curriculum that homeschool families use. So seek to know what is the best "fit" for your family and follow that with all of your heart.

Chapter 3

WHY THE LOW NUMBER OF MINORITIES?

I n 1998, Home School Legal Defense Association sponsored a research study which was conducted by Dr. Lawrence Rudner. This study showed the statistics of minorities in homeschooling. African Americans, Hispanics, Asians, Jews and Native Americans comprised 6% of the 1.3 million in the homeschooling community. This number is quite low compared to 32.8% in the public school nationally. So why this low number of minorities within the homeschooling community?

FEAR

Fear is defined as false evidence appearing real. Looking at the historical context of minorities in this country, they have overcame many hurdles. Economic, educational, and social status are some of those hurdles. That was not the case 30 years ago, when many plantations were still in full operation, or when many were underpaid because they were illegal immigrants, or when many families lived on reservations to preserve their heritage, and many were in hiding due to anti-Israeli relations. But as a nation we have come a long way.

Though many strides have been made towards progress, each race of minority still have one fear or another that impedes their start in homeschooling. Many feel they are not qualified educationally to teach their own children, or that they cannot afford to live on one income. It has been researched (personal communication) that one income families save more to better nurture their children. The fear of not giving their children all that will make them a better citizen than they as parents lurks around keeping many away from the lifestyle of homeschooling. But, the truth of the matter is that no matter who you are, we all have these fears, it is more magnified by the "enemy of our souls" to minorities based on history. The false evidence of the past, is made to appear real, that we don't have what it takes to nurture our children in all realms of their lives.

Looking back, into the different cultures around the world, parents have successfully trained children that have succeeded, so evidently the capability is there in every being that God created. Fear of the unknown has also hindered from embarking on the journey of homeschooling. Since, we have chosen to follow and live for God, then our future (the unknown) is in *His* hands. For, *He* has said in Jeremiah 29:11 that *"The thoughts I have for you are thoughts of peace, not of evil to give you an expected end"*. The expected end means the best to enrich our lives, taking care of the unknown.

LACK OF KNOWLEDGE

Hosea 4: 6 declares "my people are destroyed for lack of knowledge". Knowledge is the acquiring of truths. The acquiring process is the essence of knowledge. Without this powerful tool, one is said to be ignorant, which can be a costly thing in one's life. The presence of ignorance is a deterrent to maximizing one's potential. Many minorities are not aware of the choice of homeschooling in America today.

Talking to an editor of a well known minority magazine some years ago, confirmed the public ignorance of homeschooling as a viable option for minorities. This editor asked what is homeschooling about, it took some educating at that point. Some minorities have been made to believe that homeschooling is the same as called by public school officials when a troubled student is sent home on home study. Why, the same name is used for two different situations is appalling, yet it is the case. Many also feel that it requires so much in terms of requirements to homeschool.

In the state of Texas where we reside, the common comments from families we have guided on homeschooling have been "I can't believe that's all it takes". Acquiring of knowledge is a process and takes some initiation on the part of the seeker for knowledge. As there is public awareness that homeschooling is for all, it will become easy for minorities to acquire this truth and embrace it as the Lord leads.

Thinking back two years ago, we had a young African American journalist who interviewed us at home for our local newspaper, she said in all her years she had never heard of minorities homeschooling and she never thought it could be possible for them. She was aware of Anglos homeschooling because her boss homeschooled. This might sound insulting to some, but we recognized at that point, that ignorance has plagued our society in this regards. We then gave her a history lesson on homeschooling. The following was a comment that was sent to us by a minority who read an article from us in one of the leading homeschool magazines in our state: " I just wanted to say thank you for your work on the Minorities in Homeschooling feature. One of my only regrets about homeschooling is that it's predominantly Anglo-Saxon. I live in a small Panhandle town where there are no minorities who homeschool. Even when I was in Houston, it was almost exclusively Anglo-Saxon. I appreciated hearing that is changing somewhat."J.E.

Looking at what the Word of God had to say on child training, we see that God's principles are for all who will chose to follow, hence training our children as minorities has nothing to do with ethnic background. The knowledge is for all and there are living witnesses that it is vital in eradicating ignorance.

LACK OF SUPPORT

Homeschooling families are generally known to be self-motivators, leaders in their own right, and people with strong convictions. If this is the case, how can lack of support be a key in the low number of minority home educators? Great question, we forget that minorities have had to jump many hurdles through history that others did not have to deal with. Galatians 6: 2 talks about bearing one another's burden, hence fulfilling the law of Christ. The lack of support from fellow homeschoolers, family members as well as the public has been a contributing factor to the low number of minority home educators.

Many minorities have come across rude, superiority complex attitudes from people that probably do not know any better. We believe no one will deliberately set out to destroy another family through their comments. Many minority families have gone to homeschool events to be a blessing at that event by buying things and have had no one say a word to them throughout the time they were there. To many minorities it has meant lack of support and not been wanted. Some families have felt it is a waste of time attending any homeschool event, so they do all their shopping from their home.

In this 21st century, if we're going to see an increase in the number of minority home educators, then there will have to be a sense of support from the homeschooling community as well as the public that homeschooling is indeed for all. We have to have an open mind to all of God's people, and deliberately work at bringing all walls of partition down. To support means, to encourage the conviction or vision that one has, promote it and enlighten when necessary.

STEREOTYPE

The preconceived notion in the minds of most minorities that homeschooling is for the highly educated, six figure salaried and upper class of the society has also contributed to the low number of minority home educators.

The truth of the matter is that it takes love from parents to be effective in training productive children. Exploring the cultures of the world where homeschooling was and is still been practiced without them knowing that's what it is, it cannot be overemphasized that money, education or social status has nothing to do with hardworking and faithful families who are instilling strong family values in their children. In this day and age we have added academics to the family principles we desire as parents to instill in our children. These types of thinking are subtle deceits to rob us as minorities from the blessing that awaits us as parents when we follow God's principles of impacting our children's lives for God.

PLAYING IT BY EAR

This has contributed to the low number of minorities in home education.

Many times as minorities we play important issues by ear. Just because someone says one private school is better than any other, we go by that. Because, everyone in the family attended that school, then we play that by ear for our children. Gone are the days when you can still find things the way it was told to be.

Changes happen every second without our knowledge of them. Many have also played it by ear, because someone they knew wanted to homeschool and could not do it, that means they can't either. A well respected family were looking into home-schooling, they never thought there were success stories in homeschooling because one family they knew, their children couldn't read. To succeed in home education, playing it by ear will have to be deliberately ignored. The first step is following that instinct on the inside that says it is the way to go. There has to be a divine path to want to, rather than "someone said it's not good for my child". Another area where we play it by ear is the issue of social-ization. Many prospective home educators have not followed through because someone told them, their children will be a social misfit. That is not the case, studies and living witnesses have proven that home-schooled children have a balanced lifestyle which makes socialization easy for them.

According to research from Tufts, Cornell, Stanford and California, children are better socialized by parental example rather than by their peers. When children are socialized 95% by their peers we end up with what we call peer pressure. Socialization is not neutral by the way, it can either be positive or negative. Positive socialization is linked to family with the quantity and quality of time invested in that child. Negative socialization on the other hand is the me-first sociability born from more peer association and less parental interaction.

The final area of playing it by ear is in the sports arena. We have been made to believe that without sports a child cannot function normally. Due to this many minorities have overlooked the vital option of home education. What we're not aware of is the many rising opportunities for homeschoolers in sports. Many of our cities have leagues that are open to homeschoolers.

Established private schools are eager to allow homeschoolers to play on their team with a reasonable fee. The point of the matter is, playing it by ear robs us, of the blessings awaiting those who will dare to step out in faith.

What is so special about minorities homeschooling is the fact that only a small percentage (25%) homeschools out of over 1.9 million children that are homeschooled. This small number makes homeschooling special among minorities.

A journalist once asked how it was possible for minorities to homeschool successfully since in homes with both parents need both parents working to make ends meet. Many would have been upset at that question and canceled the interview right away. We knew it was ignorance and that we needed to do some orientation. Minority families are able to homeschool in the same way other families have been able to home-school.

Many homeschooling Hispanics, African-Americans, Asians, Native Americans, and Jews are professionals that earn enough for their families to live on one income. Many also have home-based businesses to help supplement their main income. Some families work out their schedules to ensure one parent at home during the day covering some aspects of the children's education. We've also seen families in which the mom is able to work from. To think that income is a barrier for minorities to homeschool is to allow stereotypes to guide our thinking. Our media has not done a great job in representing our entire society, hence we're left to think that the "Leave it to Beaver" lifestyle is not for minorities.

In the last four years, we've seen minority support groups established in different states. Why a minority support group? We have to understand that, many minority families need to see and fellowship with other minority homeschooling families. This interaction serves as a means of motivation for many minority families that feel they are the "only" ones homeschooling. It also helps the children know they are not alone.

The idea of a minority support group is to celebrate minority home educators and not a means of exclusiveness. It is a way to celebrate the diversity within the homeschooling community. Many of the minority support groups network from a national, regional, state and local levels to help bring a balance to their homeschooling experience. We'll talk about this more in the chapter five (Starting a minority support group).

Chapter 4

HOW MUCH DOES IT COST TO HOMESCHOOL?

According to some parents, the estimated cost of educating their children at home is about $250.00 per year. Many families may spend more on items such as packaged curriculum, private lessons (music, art, etc.) and magazine subscriptions. Be assured that the expenses will vary based on the choices you make. These include how many children you have, the types of materials and resources you use, whether one parent in a two-parent home stays home with the children or you are homeschooling as a single parent.

According to a recent survey taken by Homefire's

The Journal of Homeschooling, costs can be broken down into the following categories:

Establishing a homeschool: books about homeschooling, membership dues, associations, newsletters and conferences

Educational products/curricula: curriculum packages, textbooks, and workbooks for the core subjects (math, science, spelling, writing, grammar, social studies, fine arts, health/physical education), computer software, and audio and video cassettes.

Extracurricular classes

Memberships to museums, art galleries, etc.

Field trips

Miscellaneous costs: sports equipment, subscriptions, science equipment, phone, supplies, etc. If you are on a tight budget, don't forget the vast array of free resources available through the public libraries (visit our Libraries page for the public library in your area). Many parents use their own curriculum after their first year of homeschooling because it is less expensive than pre-packaged ones. Others explore thrift stores or check our garage sales to save money. In Texas, most local school districts do not allow homeschoolers to participate in their programs. Find out if your district allows such participation, but be prepared to follow their guidelines. As you gain experience, your expenses will decrease in some areas because you will know what does and does not work for your children.

Many people have asked about tax benefits for homeschooling. Individual homeschools are not considered non-profit organizations because they don't provide a community service to others, and it is not a business, as it does not exist to make a profit. Donations of money or educational supplies to your homeschool may not be written off your personal taxes or anyone else's. Also, there are no deductions for your child's homeschooling expenses because these areas are considered non-deductible personal living or family expenses. However, check with your tax advisor from time to time; the tax laws change frequently.

Because you tailor your homeschool curriculum to meet the needs and interests of your child, a typical budget does not exist. It is up to each individual family to determine how much of their income will be spent on educating their children. Remember that homeschooling is tailored to your family's goals, there is no set formula even on cost.

A word of caution though, avoid buying curriculum, resources and materials that you won't need. The temptation is there to think you'll buy it, because you might need it in the future. Adequate planning and budgeting can help erase some of these temptations.

Chapter 5

STARTING A MINORITY SUPPORT GROUP

Support groups have been beneficial for many homeschool families. Many feel, they don't have the time for all the activities that a support group has to offer. For some minority home educators, support groups provide a means of continual development in their homeschool experience.

A minority support group is for those families that know it is vital to their homeschool experience. Their children need to "see" other children just like them that homeschools to bring a balance to their socialization. These minority support groups are not meant to exclude anyone. Actually, we've seen one in Texas that is open to, welcoming any homeschool family that is excited about reaching out to minority home educators.

Starting a minority support takes a little bit of twist than your regular support group. Since it has a specific target audience, making the vision known in minority communities is vital to the success of a minority support group. A support group is ran totally by volunteers, meaning everyone doing their part to make it better for all to enjoy.

The first thing, is to make sure of your calling. It is no easy task leading a any group. A leader is truly a servant and not a lord over the people. When the people perceive a leader is lording over them, the margin of success is very slim. Depending on your level of relationship with God, making sure of your calling will take different forms. Some get the assurance through prayer, some through the written word of God, some through visions and dreams, some through the revealed word of God and some through godly counsel. The key thing is to ensure that you're suppose to do this. This is what will get you through during the dark formative stage.

After making sure of your calling to lead a minority support, you're ready to write down your goals and objectives. This will later form your constitution or bylaws. Who do you want to minister to? Is it an all inclusive minority support group? What is your religious stand? Do you have a place to meet outside of your home? How often do you plan to meet? Will this just be a get-together support group, or a coop group, or a field trip group or even a network group? Will you have an application for membership or not? Will you have membership dues? What will the dues be used for? Are you willing to account for the dues when requested? These and many more questions have to be answered in your goals and objectives. To give the support group an avenue for growth you as the leader have to embrace the vision of enlightening, supporting, encouraging, promoting, and motivating minority home educators as they homeschool.

You're now ready for the next step, try finding another minority home educator to share your vision with. You cannot be an island and succeed. With this "partner" you have a voice in your community or environment that there is a minority support group. Your initial meetings will be very informal. Try going to where the people are to let them know you exist. Your church might also be a starting point, to let the people know you're active.

When you about seven families, it's time to adjust your goals and objectives into your bylaws. You will need the assistance of others in leadership to steer the support group in the right direction. Determine at this point the offices you'll need in the group. President, Vice-President, Treasurer, Secretary and Editor would be your basic offices. Decide, if you want to have elections or just appoint interested families who believe in the vision and are willing to serve rather along side with you.

As you gain momentum, you can add to your activities. Another thing you might want to think about at this stage is if you want to affiliate with any other homeschool organization you feel have similar goals and objectives as you do. This could provide you with the opportunity to network at a broader level, giving you more access to national homeschool information and news.

When you have about twenty-five families, you might want to think about making the support group a nonprofit organization, unless you decide to remain a very small group. This will be helpful in properly accounting for the dues you receive and giving Uncle Sam an accurate record. The thought of making a support group nonprofit can be overwhelming, due to all the requirements and paperwork that goes with it. Some regional or state organizations might allow a support group to affiliate using a group exemption status. If this is what you decide you want to do, do your research thoroughly since it involves legal ramifications. You may also pay a tax-exempt status firm to file your nonprofit status.

As a minority support group leader, be prepared to give an answer to any one that asks of you the reason behind what you're doing. The Bible makes that very clear that as Christians we should be ready at all times to give an answer to anyone that asks from us the hope that we have. As homeschoolers we do have a hope. A hope that God will back us up as we strive to follow his commandment of training and nurturing our children. Taking total responsibility for their training. To this end do we ask every family that desires to start a minority support group this question: Why do you homeschool? Being able to provide a concise answer helps you as a leader to be focused, strong, unwavering, and fulfilled in what you're doing. One of the outlines we have provided to families desiring to start a minority support group is the following seven nuggets that we ask to be leaders to mediate upon: . We homeschool because:

- We have a conviction from God, a mandate, something from within that guides us into nurturing our children.
- We have been given grace from God to be obedient to His commandment to train our children.
- We are striving to be good stewards of what God has entrusted into our hands-our children.
- We have a glimpse of God's divine purpose for the world-the family unit.
- We are seeking for ways to be a solution rather than a problem.
- We are accepting our God-given responsibility as "role models" for our children.
- It is fun, as we learn together with our children.

It is very important for you as the leader to be confident in what you're doing first with your own children. Unknown to you, you're now a voice for home education in your area of influence. It is you that people will come to when they're thinking of doing the same thing- homeschool their children.

Being consistent is actually what bring growth to any established support group. Take your responsibility bit by bit, so that you can achieve all you have on your goals and objectives. Remember, that as a leader you are a servant.

Chapter 6

SOME EDUCATIONAL POINTERS

Most of our country's inner city public schools have a high percentage of minority students; be it Asian, Hispanic, African-American, Native American, or a Jew. Many families that decide to withdraw their children from public schools to homeschool, find themselves in a dilemma sometimes. They're faced with making educational choices, which had been made by the school's counselor and teachers. How in the world, are they to know their child's learning style, or where their children are academically. Many families that have relatives as educators feel incapable to make these decisions as well, even when their children have never attended a public school.

A simple acid test for determining personality types which leads to learning styles is what we call "True Colors. It is a very easy way to access two things : personality types and learning styles. True Colors explores the different personalities present in God's awesome creation. As minorities we need to be confident in who God has made us to be, we represent part of His diverse creation. If He meant for us to be the same He would have done that conveniently. There is cause for celebration as a minority, for it was God's intention in the first place.

True colors evolved from the work of Hippocrates in 400 B.C who found out that certain personalities tended to heal faster than some. His work has been so profound that graduating medical students still take the Hippocrates oath during their graduation. Why would we bring this up for homeschoolers ?

According to the developed work of Hippocrates in *True Colors*, there are four major personality types that can make your journey in homeschooling more enjoyable. Knowing the personality type of each one in your household, makes communication flow freely, strengthens your understanding of your children and makes your expectations realistic as it has to do with your child's life.

Gold : This refers to the personality type in which one is esteemed by being of service, appreciated for accuracy and thoroughness, validated by appreciation of service, very procedural at their work, specialize in results, have an overall mood of concern and key character trait is one of responsibility. A child that loves to plan, or serve will fall in this category. Since this type of personality values order and structure, a structured type of curriculum will work fine for a child that falls in this category. There are many curriculum providers that can help your child succeed with this personality.

Green: This refers to the personality type in which one is esteemed by having insights, appreciated for ideas and strategies, validated by affirming their wisdom, very pragmatic in their work, specialize in strategies, have an overall mood of calmness, and key character trait is one of ingenuity. A child that loves to solve mathematical problems, values logical approach to solving problems and very curious about life will fall in this category. Since this type of personality values insights, a curriculum that promotes Godly logical problem solving techniques will challenge and nurture children with this personality.

Blue: This refers to the personality type in which one is esteemed by helping people, appreciated for their unique contributions, validated by personal acceptance, very catalytic in their work, specialize in relationships, have an overall mood of commitment, and key character trait is one of authenticity.

A child that loves to make friends, help around the house without any type of prompting from parents, and exhibit lots of warmth and care will fall in this category. An interactive curriculum will nurture any child with this personality.

Orange: This refers to the personality type in which one is esteemed by being recognized, appreciated for their creativity, validated by visible results, very flexible in their work, specialize in being energetic, have an overall mood of being enthusiastic, and key character trait is one of skillfulness. A child that loves music, drawing, lots of freedom, or loves competition will fall in this category. A hands-on approach will be excellent for any child in this category.

This will be a good place to talk about learning styles. Personalities play a key role in how a child will learn or actually learns. There are primarily three types of learning styles.

1. *Auditory learners:* These learn well by hearing. Lecture type of lessons is of great benefit to children that learn this way. Learning through the use of tapes, or music is an added bonus.
2. *Visual Learners:* These learn well by seeing. They love charts, maps, or even lessons on the chalkboard. They can easily make connections in learning by what they see. They love text as well.
3. *Kinesthetic Learners:* These learn well by doing with their hands. They love an exploration approach to learning. They're good in woodworking, robotics, drawing and very creative.

HOW DO YOU ACCESS YOUR CHILD'S PROGRESS FROM TIME TO TIME?

A good way to access periodically is through testing. For families that live in states that require home-school families to register with their school districts, testing may already be a part of the services you receive, so check with your district administrator for testing information. The opinions on testing is very diverse among homeschoolers based on the state they reside in. In our state, our homeschool legislation states that : homeschools are categorized as private schools, and private schools are not regulated. Hence, there is no teacher certification requirements for parents or yearly testing requirements for homeschool students. In general, homeschoolers feel that testing should be a personal decision since they are the teachers and are fully aware of how their children are doing..

In about 26 states however, standardized testing is mandatory to ensure how homeschooled students compare to their public and private classmates. In some states, the decision on whether or not the students may continue to be homeschooled is made on the basis of the test results. On the other hand, some parents choose to test their children regardless of the issues. Due to our commitment to educate the minority community about homeschooling, we feel it necessary to provide this guide about testing in general.

WHAT ARE THE DIFFERENT TESTS AVAILABLE FOR HOMESCHOOLERS?

Standardized tests are yardsticks which are important in the educational system in America.

- *A standardized test* is uniform in all areas. It contains the same questions, is administered in the same manner, is completed in the same amount of time and is graded or scored using the same method.
- *An achievement test* measures a student's acquired knowledge, or past learning, in one or more areas and compares the results with a national reference group.
- *An aptitude test* measures a student's potential for future learning or performance. The difference between standardized tests is the way in which test results are compared. Some tests are *criterion referenced* while others are *norm referenced*. In a criterion referenced test, a student's test score is compared to test scores of other children. The results then shows, whether the student exceeds, meets, or falls below the established proficiency level in a given subject area. In a norm referenced test, the student's test score is compared to a sample of children or select "norm group" usually within the same age and

grade level. The test scores indicate what percentage of children scored at or below the student's score.

TYPE OF TESTS

- **ITBS** (Iowa Test of Basic Skills), this test measures a variety of skills and content areas, including reading, language arts, mathematics, social studies, science, and information sources that are considered essential to a child's education
- **MAT** (Metropolitan Achievement Test), this test measures student achievement, or mastery of content, in five disciplines: reading, mathematics, science, language arts, and social studies as well as thinking and reasoning skills.
- **SAT**(Stanford Achievement Test), this test is a battery or group of related tests combining achievement and aptitude tests using both criterion and norm referenced for comparisons. *This is different from the well-known SAT test for college entrance exam-Scholastic Assessment Test.*
- **CogAt**(Cognitive Abilities Test), this test assesses a student's abilities in reasoning and problem solving using verbal, quantitative and spatial, or nonverbal symbols. It is normally administered with the ITBS test.

- **OLSAT** (Otis-Lennon School Ability Tests), this test measures reasoning and complex thinking skills. It is normally administered with the SAT test-Standard Achievement Test.
- **CAT** (California Achievement Tests), this test assesses academic achievement of students in the areas of reading, language arts, mathematics, social studies and science.

HOMESCHOOLERS AND TESTING

According to a 1998 study authored by University of Maryland professor Lawrence M. Rudner, who was at that time director of the Education Resources Information Center (ERIC) Clearinghouse on Assessment and Evaluation, homeschooled children score well above the national median on standardized tests. Bob Jones University Press Testing and Evaluation service provides homeschool families access to standardized achievement tests. Students who have been homeschooled their entire academic lives have higher scholastic achievement test scores than those who have attended other educational programs or who have been homeschooled for only a few years. Almost one-fourth of homeschooled students (24.5%) is studying at one or more grade levels above their normal or age-appropriate grade. By eighth grade, the average homeschooled student performs four grade level above the national average.

How about homeschooling and your gifted child? Giftedness covers a wide range of a child's abilities and needs. Children who are gifted come in all shapes and sizes, and have their own individual characteristics. They also have the same basic needs as other children, and uniqueness as all children do.

Issues and concerns that apply to gifted children apply to homeschooled gifted children as well. Many supporters of homeschooling are not all for testing due to labeling, governmental interference and other issues. However, identifying gifted, homeschooled children is good so that their special needs can be met.

In a typical classroom setting, researchers recommend an educational plan that is individualized, flexible, challenging with parental involvement, based on life experiences and the child's interests. Well, that just described homeschooling in all aspects. If researchers can come up with "a homeschooling plan" to nourish gifted children, then we have a greater edge as homeschoolers in the real sense to meet all the needs of a gifted child.

Instead of going through the normal 12 years of standardized curriculum and risking the loss of interest in learning or developing underachieving children, homeschooling is better suited to the individual gifted child. Homeschooling gives the benefit of putting the emphasis on the child rather than the curriculum. Gifted children learn best when they are challenged and have success in learning. Because they function at an advanced developmental stage in one or more areas, a well-designed curriculum is very important. It should broaden interest, explore topics in-depth, allow for review of materials at an accelerated and compact pace, and include enrichment activities based on interests.

Here are some things to consider if you are homeschooling a gifted child or plan to homeschool a gifted child

- Consider using the expertise of mentors, apprenticeships or tutors in some areas of your child's development
- Avoid constant repetition of concepts that your child have mastered, rather give special projects around those mastered concepts
- Build on the strengths of the child rather than weaknesses
- Limit competitive situations
- Include your child when designing the curriculum, ask for their interests
- Allow the child to advance at his/her own pace
- Provide adequate downtime of reflection and relaxation
- Provide learning materials all around the home that is above the child's cognitive level.

A parent does not have to be gifted to teach a gifted child. However, to encourage growth and development, you must have a thorough understanding of giftedness and a solid commitment to educating the whole child (spirit, soul and body). Homeschooling, provides a balanced instruction for a gifted child to soar high and realize and reach his or her potential.

WHAT IS GIFTEDNESS BY THE WAY?

Giftedness can be defined as a situation in which a child or youth exhibits high performance capability in areas such as intellectual, creative, artistic, or leadership capacity, or in specific academic fields. Such child/youth many times needs many activities to fully develop such capabilities. Identifying gifted children is not an easy process. Not all gifted children are achievers, some perform exceptionally well, while others are just average, and still some are learning disabled.

A variety of ways is needed to identify giftedness, IQ testing is not sufficient. Characteristics of gifted children, parental observations, creative and critical thinking tests, IQ testing measuring verbal, nonverbal, mathematical reasoning, and short term memory, are some ways of accessing and identifying giftedness. According to the National Association of Gifted Children, there are five different areas of giftedness:

1) **Visual/performing arts:** This includes an outstanding sense of spatial relationships; unusual ability for expression through art, dance, drama and music; good motor coordination; creative expression; and a desire for producing original materials.

2) **Leadership:** This includes fluent self-expression, good judgment and organizational skills, self-confidence, responsibility, and generally have the high respect of their peers.

3) **Creative thinking:** This includes improvising, having a keen sense of humor, creativity, and inventiveness, original thinking in oral and written expression, and being unique.

4) **General intellectual ability:** This includes the ability in having a wide range of information, high levels of vocabulary, memory, abstract word knowledge, and abstract thinking.

5) **Specific Academic ability:** This involves high academic success in one area such as math or science, acquiring of basic skill knowledge quickly, and having advanced comprehension and possessing good memorization ability.

Some characteristics of gifted children include several of the following:

- Abstract reasoning and problem-solving skills
- Exhibiting advanced progression through developmental milestones
- Possess vivid imagination

- Learns quickly and easily
- Pursues an interest or hobby intensively for a time
- Absorbs large amounts of information quickly and recalls accurately and easily
- Perform complicated mathematics from memory
- Shows outstanding curiosity, initiative, or insight, asks lots of questions
- Has a large vocabulary and uses words effectively
- Reads at a very early age
- Shows a keen sense of humor

Remember that to fully develop the giftednes in your child requires a lot of dedication, love and solid commitment. As Christian parents, asking God for wisdom daily to direct the education of your children is vital in fully training each child to be all that God has destined them to be.

BUILDING WRITING SKILLS

The office of Educational Research and Improvement released an article in April of 1993 that addresses how parents in general can help their children of all ages learn how to write well.

Writing is more than putting words on paper. It's final stage is the complex process of communicating that begins with "thinking." Writing is an important stage in communication, the intent being to leave no room for doubt. Has any country ratified a verbal treaty?

One of the first means of communication for your child is through drawing. Do you encourage the child to draw and to discuss his/her drawings. Ask questions : What is the boy doing? Does the house look like ours? Can you tell a story about this picture?

Most children's basic speech patterns are formed by the time they are school age. By that time children speak clearly, recognize most letters of the alphabet, and may try to write. show an interest in, and ask questions about, the things your child says, draws, and may try to write.

Writing well requires:

- Clear thinking
- Sufficient time
- Reading
- Meaningful task (a child needs meaningful, not artificial writing tasks)
- Interest
- Practice and more practice

POINTERS FOR PARENTS

In helping your child to learn to write well, remember that your goal is to make writing easier and more enjoyable.

- Provide a good place to write with good lighting

- Have the materials available-paper, pencils, etc.
- Allow time for thinking about a writing project or exercise. Good writers do a great deal of thinking. Be patient.
- Respond verbally to their ideas.
- Praise your child's work.

Jacqueline Pearce, who is a Reading and Writing Specialist in Dallas, wrote an article to help parents with ideas for writing projects. Here is an except from that article:

As we work with young people around writing, two main goals appear:

- To help our child or student develop excellence in his or her writing and
- To inspire our child or student to love writing. The ideas listed below can help your children achieve these two goals.

TOPICS FOR YOUNG CHILDREN (AGES FOUR TO SEVEN):

Write a story about:

- yourself
- your family
- your favorite toy
- your favorite part of a story
- how you would have solved a recent problem.

- how you would have solved a problem in a story
- a recipe for a sandwich or other food item
- a how-to paragraph for brushing your teeth, getting ready for bed, getting dressed, eating breakfast or going to the grocery store.

TOPICS FOR OLDER WRITERS

(1) Write a story from the point of view of an object you use, e.g.., your sneaker, your front door, a book you read. Talk about a day in the life of your object.

(2) Write a new ending for your favorite story. Place your favorite story in a new setting. How would it change? How would the characters, problems, or resolutions change? If you could be one of the characters in a story, who would you be? Why? Is there a character in the story who is similar to you?

(3) Write about your similarities and differences. Is there a character in your story that is similar to a member of your family? How so?

RESEARCH

(1) Research a country and create a travel brochure for it. The travel brochure must include pertinent information: what would that be? What would you want to know before you went there?

(2) Create a two or three day itinerary. Where would you go, and why? Write a persuasive essay to convince travelers to take your tour.

(3) Research a pioneer - a pioneer in any field, be it sports, medicine, science, religion, etc. Discover as much as you can about his or her motivation. Search until you find the ways he or she surmounted the obstacles in his or her path. Describe what distinguished this person from his or her peers. If this person is still alive, write a letter to him or her.

Children want to be heard, and often feel more motivated to write when they know they will have an audience. Some possible audiences are:

- residents of a nursing home
- a church group
- younger siblings
- their friends
- grandparents

- their pets
- a librarian
- your homeschooling group

IMPROVING SPELLING SKILLS

Do you want to improve your spelling while having fun? Here's a fun game to play- Hangman. Draw a picture like the one below without the stick man and place the number of blank spaces for your mystery word (this example is shepherd). As the participants guess letters for the word, either fill in the blank spaces with the correct letters or draw a part of the stick man for each missed letter (for example, if someone guessed "Q" for this example, draw a head or foot or leg, etc.) The participants win if they guess the word before the complete picture of the man is drawn.

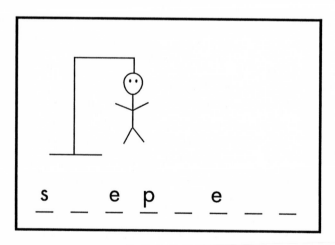

How about Science? This is question is common among homeschool families. Science is all around us, a means for us as homeschool parents to give our children an appreciation of God's creation. Science is best learnt when a child can see it, touch it, feel it and do it. Below is an except from one of our designed science curriculum that you can use to introduce your child to the world of science.

BRANCHES OF SCIENCE

Introduction. God is the ultimate source of knowledge. Hence science demonstrates God's ability in man. Science comes from the *Latin* word *"scientia"*(sigh' en tee uh) which means to have knowledge.

I. **The Sciences can be divided into 2 main groups:**
    A. Pure Natural Sciences
    B. Applied Sciences

II. **The Pure Natural Sciences** :This is divided into 6 branches
    A. **Physics-**study of all the physical sciences
    B. **Astronomy-**study of the stars, space and the galaxies
    C. **Chemistry-**study of solutions, mixtures and it's chemical entities
    D. **Botany-**study of plant and its entities
    E. **Zoology-**study of animals and its entities

F. **Geology**-study of rocks and its entities

III. **The Applied Sciences**
A. **Aeronautic**s-study of the forces of wind as it relates to aviation
B. **Electronics**-study of the electric aspect of science
C. Engineering-study of ....?........ (find out)
D. Agronomy-study of ....?........ (find out)
E. Social science- study of ......?..... (find out).
F. Behavioral science-study of ......?... (find out)
G. Technology- study of ....?...... (find out)

PROCESS SKILLS

Process skills are the skills which are used commonly in Science during investigation or laboratory experiments. There are five process skills that are used in any science investigation. Observation, Classification, Measurement, Prediction and Communication. The best way to master these process skills is through "doing". The following is a very simple experiment to introduce your child to the use of process skills. You may repeat the experiment as many times as you need to help your child master process skills.

PENNY LAB

You will need 10 pennies, a ruler, a dropper, paper towels and a piece of paper to record your findings.

- OBSERVE: Take one penny and lay it with the front facing you (Head-In God we trust). *Look at* it: What is it's color, size, shape and any other characteristics? Describe your penny using 2/3/4 sentences.

- CLASSIFY: Now place your 10 pennies *in order*

    1) from dullest to shiniest-draw each one and write the date below each one.
    2) from oldest to newest. Write the date inside each drawing of penny .
    3) *Sort* the pennies by the "D" stamped under the date. Find out what "D" means. How many pennies with a "D"? How many pennies without a "D".

- MEASURE: Using a ruler, measure the *diameter* of your penny.

    1) The diameter is .... mm.
    2) Stack your pennies to equal 1 cm. How many pennies equal 1 cm?

3) Use your penny as a unit of measure-ment. How many pennies *long* or *wide* are the following objects.

   a) The length of your pennies = ... pennies

   b) The width of your wrist = ... pennies

   c) The length of your shoe = ... pennies

   d) The length of your little finger = ... pennies.

- PREDICTING: *Guess* how many drops of water can fit the top of a penny with-out spilling, write it down. Now, place a penny on the paper towel, how many drops of water can fit on the top of a penny without spilling? When the paper towel becomes wet, you know that you have spilled the water.

Trial	Prediction	Results
1		
2		
3		

- COMMUNICATING: Have someone describe the building on the back of the penny. Try and draw the building from their directions.

Draw with directions	Draw looking at the penny

SCIENTIFIC METHOD

This is the writing style used in explaining scientific experiments or investigations. It is a systematic approach to problem-solving with six major steps.

PROBLEM: State this in a sentence

GATHERING INFORMATION: All available information related to the problem must be gathered.

HYPOTHESIS: Suggest a possible solution to the problem

EXPERIMENT: Perform experiment according to specific rules. Variable, this is the factor that is being tested. The stable factor is the control. Materials used should be included in this step.

RESULTS: Observe during experiment, and record all your findings. Recorded observations and measurements makes your DATA.

CONCLUSION: Was the hypothesis correct or not?

PRACTICE USING THE SCIENTIFIC METHOD

A) Think of a problem you will like to solve as a young scientist. Using the Scientific Method write your report.

B) Each sentence below describes a step of the scientific method. Match each sentence with a step of the scientific method listed below.
  A. recognize a problem
  B. form a hypothesis
  C. Experiment
  D. make a conclusion

.... 1. Steven predicted that seeds would start to grow faster if an electric current traveled through the soil in which they were planted.

.... 2. Maya said, " If I fertilize my geranium plants, they will blossom"

.... 3.   Jon's data showed that household roaches moved away from raw onion slices.

.... 4.   Irene grew bacteria from the mouth on special plates in the lab. She placed drops of different mouthwash on bacteria on each plate.

.... 5.   Kelly wanted to know how synthetic fibers were different from natural fibers.

.... 6.   Willie wondered if dyes could be taken out of plant leaves, flowers, and stems.

.... 7.   Lola read about growing plants in water. She wanted to know how plants could grow without soil.

.... 8.   Armon experimented with the diets of guinea pigs. He found that guinea pigs need vitamin C and protein in their diets.

.... 9.   Liberty used a survey to determine how many of her friends were left-handed and how many were right-handed.

.... 10. Evan saw bats catching insects after dark. He asked, "How do bats find the insects after dark?"

Chapter 7

HOMESCHOOL LEGISLATION

We are a living witness to how information can help make a better decision. Hence, we have included this chapter with the help of the *Home School Legal Defense Association*. Take a look at each summary laws of all the 50 states, at the Appendix and be better informed as you make decisions toward homeschooling. You will find out what the requirements are in your home state. Please, be advised that this chapter does not constitute legal advise, it is only for your information. For legal advise contact your attorney or join Home School Legal Defense Association, their contact information is 540-338-5600.

Many of the states that show favor to homeschoolers, has been largely due to participation of homeschoolers in their democratic government. Participation in form of voting and electing legislators to various offices. It has also been due to their obedience to the command given to us in the Bible to pray for our leaders in government.

Every legislative session, bills are formulated that affect one way or the other the freedom of homeschoolers to continue in their God given calling to train their children.

This chapter is also a wake up call to us as homeschoolers, no matter our background or ethnicity we have a responsibility to pray for our government.

We can be involved right from where we are. Ensuring the publication of homeschool friendly articles in our local/community newspaper, is a step in the right direction. Sharing our success stories can affect legislation as well.

Responding to prompts from your local homeschool group, when there is a challenge facing homeschoolers in the legislation also counts for participation.

At the end of this book we have included the facts provided by Home School Legal Defense Association to help you know the laws of homeschooling in every state. This appendix does not constitute legal advise.

Chapter 8

TESTIMONIALS

I t is very true that when you find someone that has trod the path you're looking forward to treading, a confidence arises from within you. This more or less gives you a point of reference so to speak. The various families you'll meet in this chapter are in the mainstream of homeschooling. But what is interesting is the uniqueness of each family. Homeschooling is a lifestyle that should be tailored to fit your family uniqueness, for indeed each family is unique, a special design of God to make us appreciate His creation.

THE CRAIGS

Charles, a full-time pastor, and Janice who has a background in nursing, home school their nine children(3 girls and 6 boys). While the Craig's daughter earned every first grade award at a Christian school, their 5-year-old son was not ready to sit quietly for educational disciplines. A teacher relative of the family confirmed that an alarming number of black boys was skidding into educational doldrums by upper elementary years. This enigma concerning their son's education was the dominant catalyst that spurred the Craigs into the uncharted home school waters in 1984. Never doubting their children's educational prowess, they were uncertain about how institutions of higher learning would accept their novel education. Their four graduates have fared admirably. Their first child is now in medical school in Texas, the second one is an apprentice computer LANs server, another is a master barber, and the fourth graduate is an education major in college.

THE HAUGABOOKS

Tommy and Rhonda Haugabook have been homeschooling for the past ten years. In addition to Tommy, who serves as dad and principal and is the owner of T. Haugabook Services, and Rhonda, mother and teacher, who is certified instructor with BS in home & family sciences, the family is made up of their 14 year-old son who is a ninth grader, and 8 year-old daughter who is in the fourth grade. The Haugabooks main reasons for homeschooling were a desire for excellence and a deep passion for God to be included in every facet of their lives. Being African-Americans, they also wanted their children to be exposed to and take pride in African history, recognizing theirs as a dynamic race of beings created by the Almighty God. They have enjoyed the obstacles as well as the triumphs that come with homeschooling since they began in 1989. They believe that homeschooling is the only choice to guarantee their children's success.

THE WELLS

Kennard Wells, an MD-88 captain for one of US major airlines, and his wife Georgette, a social worker, homeschool their 8 year-old daughter and 4 year-old son. When their daughter's experience in a private school did not prove to be what she needed, her parents made the decision to homeschool. Her love for learning has been renewed, and her skills in math, reading, writing, and public speaking have greatly improved in the homeschooling setting.

THE JOHNSONS

The Johnson Christian Academy was established in 1989 by parents/teachers James and Felecia. They have five children ages: 14, 12, 10, 8(a special needs child) and 6. James is a senior director of support services for a major networking company and Felecia was a licensed hair designer before homeschooling. Their decision to homeschool was brought about by their concerns about both how the public school teachers would keep their bright, active daughter busy for eight hours daily and how their Christian values would not be upheld. Over the past ten years of their homeschooling, there have been many success stories for them, but the one that stands out in their minds is the in-depth understanding that their daughter now enjoys in math. She hated math; now in the ninth grade, she understands algebra better than her mother. She has plans to study advanced math and she now tutors her friends in math.

THE HERNANDEZES

Juan and Salustia Hernandez are the parents of two children. The older child is in 12th grade and the younger one is in the 7th grade. After being let down by the school system in which their children were enrolled, these parents in a bilingual home decided that homeschooling would provide both a better way of life and a quality means of education for their children. Today they have hope and see progress in the making in their children's academic skills. This was contrary to the despair they once had when their children were in public school.

THE ODOMS

The Odoms are a family of six. Fred is a seminary student and a full-time quality assurance monitor for an entertainment company, Eileen is a full-time manager at home. God has blessed them with four active, intelligent children to nurture and teach for Him.

Their initial homeschooling decision was based on economic barriers to Christian school and concerns about the quality of public education in their inner-city community. They researched homeschooling and sought advice from veteran homeschoolers. Currently, they have their two older children in a Christian school that provides African-American cultural context. The two younger ones get all their education from home. They initially had concerns about socialization for one of the younger ones, but with opportunities for socialization from their church, ballet, and homeschool group activities, she continues to blossom.

THE OBAMEHINTIS

Johnson a professional Veterinary Nutritionist with the Dallas Zoo, and wife, Feyi a certified teacher with bachelors in microbiology and masters in science education, homeschool their three children- Lola, Layo and Lade. Having a strong-willed daughter, who showed great intellectual competence at age 2, led them into homeschooling. She and her sisters started reading fluently at age 3. Knowing that God had blessed them with intellectually gifted children, they desired to balance that gift with godly character and wanted to provide the environment (their home) for them to flourish. Looking back, they can see a godly lady in the making in Lola, and are thankful for the privilege of homeschooling. Their choice in home education is something they are thankful for- because it was God's desire that became their choice.

THE WILLIAMS

Through the experiences of this entrepreneurial family, they are re-educating themselves with every class that is done for their two sons in their homeschooling environment. Their decision to homeschool came from their despair with the school systems. Their homeschooling experience has also made it possible to see themselves in their children.

WHAT PEOPLE ARE SAYING ABOUT THE VISION OF SUPPORTING MINORITY HOME EDUCATORS

The vision of ministering to minority home educators has touched many lives. Here are some of the comments about how this vision has affected the lives and lifestyles of others.

I am Hispanic and married to an Anglo. I do appreciate what you are doing with ministering to minority home educators because I have encountered, many times, objections and critical attitudes toward my homeschooling choice (Hispanics and other minorities); and all I can say is that it is due to a lack of education on the subject.

—San Antonio, TX

God is so good. We are thrilled to learn that there is something like this. We are excited to learn about your organization as a resource to pass information on to others, starting at our church.

—Chicago, IL

I haven't yet decided on homeschooling, but I have been toying with the idea for some time. My son will start in the fall of 2002, and I'm just not sure I'm ready to hand him over to the world. I enjoy being at home with him and his sister, being their main source for learning manners, education, and spiritual guidance. I'm glad that if I take the home-school journey, that support will be there for me!

—Garland, TX

I was blessed to hear that God had laid it on someone's heart to start a homeschool group for minorities. It has always bothered me that my children and I would always be the only minority in the homeshcool groups in the past, and I always believed that more of us needed to know that we are capable of homeschooling, also, if that's what God has called us to do.

—Ft. Worth, TX

The minority support group in Dallas has opened my family's eyes to the many opportunities that are available to homeschoolers. We fee secure, and there is no need to keep silent anymore. The vision has been a great source of support to our family. After every monthly meeting, I am motivated, all over again, knowing that there is a great reward at the end of the tunnel.

—Seagoville, TX

My name is Tracy. I myself am adopted, but my son is not.; He is from a mixed marriage where I am white and his father is Black, with a bit of native

American.; My son has been to a mixture of racial environments and also around those who are special needs folks with various disabilities or other issues.; I am now a single parent, but the dad is still involved in his son's life so that is a plus.. As my son was a toddler I did not tell him he was black, brown or anything else, but when he began to learn his colors he told my mother and I that we were either yellow or orange since he got the colors mixed up. Then as he grew to age three and went to a preschool class he learned from others that he was "black", however he got the colors; brown and black mixed up then.; My son also went with me on my delivery jobs until he was out of his car seat and began public school.. We went to different folks, mainly the white upper class neighborhoods. He had been around white kids primarily in our babysitting coops, and he got along well with other kids from all economic backgrounds. It wasn't until we went to the black side of town that my son noticed the old buildings and the way people dressed and walked around in their community that he noticed that they were black, like his grandma Betty. First he asked me if all of these people were grandma Betty's family. I told him no. Then he said something that stays with me that only a 4 year old would say with an air of I declare..."Well, someone took away all their food." He and I had just come from the wealthy side of town delivering the restaurant meals we delivered then, and he noticed the difference between wealth and poverty. Later, we moved into that area and found lots of good neighbors, and a culture in the black community unique to Austin, Texas. We participated in the marches for

Lacresha Murray the day we decided for sure we were going to homeschool. Not bad for citizenship when the kid got front page on a newspaper for his sign he drew for the march. We have found there is a definite culture, where at times my son doesn't like being black. At other times I try to instill in him a knowledge of history, both pro and con, and positive role models in history. It is of interest to me to learn about slavery and my own family history. How do we deal with that in teaching about mankind? My church has its own ethnic histories that needs to be explored and researched. There is so much we could be doing for the world by simply doing our genealogy and researching history to keep it alive in the form of curriculums for the next generations of all homeschoolers. So many homeschoolers are in acting, and I am thankful for their contributions to historical and other film making. I hope you don't mind if I add your list to my bookmark pages, because the value of what you have given to Texas homeschoolers and others is so important.. Thank you for your email group. I look forward to hearing more from this group.

The ministry of supporting minority home educators has challenged us to go further and search for more. It has also created a "bar" by which we are able to measure where we are and where we should be.

—Dallas, TX

Some of these comments you may find in full on our website at www.mhot.org (Minority Homeschoolers of Texas)

Chapter 9

THE NEED FOR PUBLIC AWARENESS

There is a great need for public awareness that homeschooling is really for all. If there has ever been a time when parents need to stand up for what they believe it is now. Failure to stand up for something, will make it easy to fall for anything.

The public need awareness that homeschooling is not a form of neglect as many have claimed it to be. Homeschooled children are trained academically, socially and spiritually to meet the demands of our society. According to an article published by Investors Business Daily in 1999, homeschooled children score much higher than the national average, even higher than kids at private school. Published in this article was the thorough study of homeschooling that appeared in the journal Education Policy Analysis Archives done by Lawrence Rudner, a statistician at the University of Maryland, he looked at standardized test scores of more than 20,000 homeschooled children. This article also, showed the type of training homeschoolers are exposed to; in which they are more likely to take part in civic activities, such as volunteering or joining community organizations.

The public need awareness that homeschooling parents have not lost their minds just because they chose to train their children at home versus public education. Extended family members need to be educated about homeschooling. Many of the battles homeschoolers have faced in the past have come directly or indirectly from extended family members.

The public need awareness that as minorities we have not betrayed the system by homeschooling. Many have argued why homeschool as a minority since the public schools was a major provision for minorities and the fact that through civil rights public education was desegregated to allow minorities to have access to quality education. To appreciate the diversity God has created, there is the need to steer clear of a "one size fits all" mentality. Why would there be a claim that, you can only have a quality education through public education, neither to say, home education is the only way for education. Home education is an alternative to public education.

Some of the ways we can provide public awareness is through the public libraries. Information packets can be placed in every local library to help educate the public about homeschooling. Check with your librarian on how to go about doing this. many of the libraries love homeschooling families, because they are avid readers and make use of the library very often.

Another way is by writing articles in your local newspapers on homeschooling. Approach your local newspaper editor on how to do this.

Approaching your local radio stations to place announcements on the community bulletin board is also very helpful in making the community aware that minorities do homeschool. Placing these announcements during specific celebrations like Black history month, Cinco de Mayo will help the public realize the richness of celebrating cultural heritage by minority homeschoolers.

Placing information packets in your local chambers of commerce helps to broaden the minds of the public about homeschooling. It will be a great resource for the Asian, Black or Hispanic chambers of commerce.

One of the most beneficial ways for public awareness is having a minority homeschool support group in your community. The many testimonials of families who have been enriched, strengthened by been an active participant of such a group can not be overemphasized. Cultural heritage program in such groups have made history lessons come alive for many.

One family shared their story with us: They have homeschooled for four years their only teenage daughter. She told her parents that homeschooling was just for Anglos and not for her, since she has never met other homeschooled teenager that looked like her. When they became a part of a minority support group, they could notice the change in attitude in their daughter. She is now in her senior year in high school still homeschooling. She has been able to make friends that she believes will last a long time.

Chapter 10

WHERE CAN I FIND CURRICULUM?

The homeschool market has exploded in the last ten years with resources to help parents in their call to home educate their children. We have selected from a wide variety and these are some resources to help the new homeschooler in their journey or to enhance a veteran homeschooler. As you would any important step in your life, make every effort to research before purchasing any material. Most of the curriculum providers below, have toll free numbers that you can call and request for their free catalog to be sent to you. This way you are not under any pressure to buy, rather to research which ones best meet your homeschool style.

CURRICULUM

1. A Beka Book: Christian textbooks, curriculum and support materials 1-877-223-5226
2. Alpha Omega: Provides Christian homeschool curricula, in a user-friendly format. 1-877-688-2652
3. Bob Jones University Press: Christian textbooks, curriculum, support materials and Video school. 1-800-845-5731
4. Calvert School: Calvert school offers a complete fully accredited curriculum for Pre-kindergarten through Grade Eight. 1-888-487-4652
5. Curriculum Services: Complete, parent-friendly, K-12 program with over eighteen years of experience. 1-877-702-1419
6. ESP Books: Creators of the world famous Golden Year Books. 1-800-643-0280
7. How Great Thou Art: A Godly perspective on art. 1-800-982-DRAW
8. The Jason Project: The Jason Project has helped put adventure and excitement of discovery into science education. 1-888-527-6600
9. Keystone National High School: An independent study specialist for over twenty-five years. 1-800-255-4937
10. School of Tomorrow: Parent-friendly curriculum for K-12. 1-800-925-7777
11. Self-Teaching Robinson Curriculum: 250 books and exams in 22 CD-ROMS. 1-248-740-2697
12. The Noah Plan: A complete educational program in The Principle Approach. 1-800-352-FACE

INDEPENDENT STUDY

1. Alger Learning Center: Nationally accredited and specializing in working with students who want to design their own curriculum. 1-800-595-2630
2. University of Florida Correspondence Study: Quality Education..anytime.. and anywhere. 1-800-327-4218

PRIVATE DISTANCE-LEARNING SCHOOLS (ELEMENTARY)

1. Alpha Omega Academy On-line: Offers computer based education for parents who are wanting to homeschool, yet are looking for the teaching and benefits of a private school. 1-877-688-2652
2. Clonlara: All the benefits of home education and the support of a private school. 1-734-769-4511
3. Laurel Springs School: Accredited K-12 Distance Learning Program offering teachers that provide a flexible curriculum sensitive to each students individual learning styles. 1-800-377-5890

PRIVATE DISTANCE-LEARNING SCHOOLS (HIGH SCHOOL)

1. Alpha Omega On-line: Offers computer based education. 1-877-688-2652
2. Indiana University High School: Fully accredited by the North Central association of Colleges and Schools. 1-800-334-1011

3. Laurel Springs School: Accredited K-12 Distance Learning Program. 1-800-377-5890

TEST PREPARATION

1. Perfection Learning: Test preparation for grades 3-12. 1-800-762-2999
2. Regents College: Excellent tools for helping homeschooled students demonstrate college level readiness and knowledge. 1-888-RCEEXAMS

ONLINE LEARNING/INTERNET SUPPORT

1. ChildU: Interactive K-6 curriculum. 1-877-4childU
2. PCS Edventures: Internet-delivered educational program designed for families with children ages 6 and up. 1-800-429-3110
3. FamilyConnect: Provides a family-safe internet access. 1-888-400-0239
4. HomeSchool Family Network: A dedicated ISP for helping you educate and protect your children while they surf. 1-888-811-4785

MATH

1. Math Concepts: Get your children excited about math.1-800-574-9936
2. Saxon Math: Build your child's confidence in math, curriculum for K-12. 1-800-284-7019

3. Scholastix Software: A comprehensive math software, helps propel a child's desire for math through games and step-by-step graphics that cover all of basic math. 1-888-675-7948

SCIENCE:

1. American Science and Surplus: Offers science kits, educational toys, school supplies, arts and crafts items, hobby tools, scales, lab gloves, housewares, electronics and much more-all at discount prices. 1-847-982-0870
2. Edventures.com: This is an internet-delivered educational program designed for families with children ages 6 and up. 1-800-429-3110
3. Interactive Learning, Inc.: Interactive software for Biology, Chemistry and Physics. 1-877-472-3371
4. Science Kit and Boreal Laboratories: Award winning microscopes and more. 1-800-828-7777

LANGUAGE ARTS

1. Earobics: Software that teaches phonemic awareness, auditory processing introductory phonics skills needed to learn to read and spell 1-847-328-8099
2. Frontline Phonics: Start early and give your child the reading edge. 1-800-584-READ
3. Getty-Dubay: The italic handwriting series for kindergarten to 6th graders. 1-800-547-8887 x 4891

4. Hooked On Phonics: a proven system that can help your child become a better, more confident reader in as little as 4 weeks. 1-800-532-3607

5. Inspired Idea: Innovative Christ-centered learning with Unblocked-the dysgraphia workbook (for the child who can't write), Color Phonics, Rev-Up for Reading, Rev-Up for Writing and more. 1-480-940-6147

6. Perfection Learning: Literature tests, Grammar Works and Hi-Low Readers for reluctant readers. 1-800-8311-4190

7. Saxon Phonics: Saxon Phonics encourages and provides the skills for children to become lifelong readers. 1-800-284-7019

8. Writing Strands: Writing Strands is the leading, award winning curriculum designed especially for homeschoolers. 1-800-688-5375

FOREIGN LANGUAGE COURSES

1. The Learnables: Easy to use self-study language tapes/books available in Spanish, French, German, Russian, Japanese, Chinese, Hebrew, Czech English as a foreign language. 1-800-237-1830

2. Muzzy, the BBC Language Course for Children: A complete multimedia program available today to teach your child Spanish, French, German or Italian. 1-888-248-0480

MISCELLANEOUS

1. How Great Thou Art : A Godly perspective on Art. 1-800-982-DRAW
2. Meet the Masters: Interactive art education that brings out the creativity in K-8 students. 1-949-492-1583
3. Regents College: Regents College Examination are excellent tools for helping homeschooled students demonstrate college level readiness and knowledge. 1-888-RCEXAMS
4. Prufrock Press: The leading publisher for gifted and talented education. 1-800-998-2208
5. Classroom Visuals: Provider of a complete educational video membership service. 1-888-560-4787
6. Growing Without Schooling Magazine: A great magazine for parents seeking alternatives to conventional schooling. 1-888-925-9298
7. Home Education Magazine: A great resource for any homeschooling family 1-800-236-3278
8. Homeschoolers Supply: Offers a variety of hands-on learning toys and games, specifically selected for homeschoolers-a combination of FUN and FAMILY VALUES. 1-877-746-3069
9. Special Needs: Disability and Business Technical Assistance Centers 1-800-949-4232-This is a great source for information and training on the Americans with Disabilities Act. There are ten centers across the country, each serving a regional collection of states.
10. The Dyslexic Reader Newsletter-1-888-999-3324

BOOKFAIRS

Bookfairs are your one stop in finding curriculum for your homeschool program. It features a variety of exhibitors and choices for your needs. Check with your local or regional support group for bookfairs in your area.

ABOUT THE
AUTHORS

Johnson and Feyi Obamehinti have been married for thirteen years, and have three wonderful girls: Lola, Layo and Lade. They have homeschooled for ten years (and plan on homeschooling their girls to college level) , utilizing different methods from, private school, umbrella schooling, correspondence, coop to independent approach. Their children are actively involved in the community and are recipients of various awards.

Johnson was born into a Muslim royal family and raised by Muslim parents, learning the tenets of the Muslim religion in Nigeria, Africa. At age 15 he was allowed to attend a Christian school, and there he began to thirst for more, the Muslim religion became distasteful to him. On November 14, 1977, he found the answer to his long quest, he was in need of a Savior. Responding to the altar call of a traveling evangelist to his home town, who had just finished preaching about the Saving Grace of God in His Son Jesus Christ, Johnson gave his life to Jesus Christ. It was evident, that God's hand was upon him. In fulfillment of a given prophesy, Johnson came to the U.S as a missionary, with a mission to evangelize, impact his neighborhood, workplace, church and support the vision of his covering pastor.

Today, Johnson is the *Veterinary Nutritionist* for the Dallas Zoo in Texas, one of few Wildlife nutritionist in the country and the only African American to practice successfully in that profession. He holds an undergraduate and graduate degrees in Animal Science & Nutrition, holds many professional licenses from the American Zoo and Aquarium Association, Nutrition Advisory Group, American Society of Animal Science, Texas Animal Nutrition Council, and Wildlife Conservation Council. He is also an ordained minister of the gospel, founder and president of the Minority Homeschoolers of Texas and it's subsidiaries (Minority Homeschoolers of Dallas Metroplex), the first established minority homeschool organization in Texas, Minority Homeschoolers of Houston and with MHSA in the making.

Feyi was born in Phoenix, Arizona and raised in a Christian home in Nigeria, Africa. She gave her life to Jesus Christ at age 15. She holds a BS in Microbiology, masters in Science Education, Curriculum Developer, and a Texas State Certified

Secondary Composite Science teacher. She is also an ordained minister of the gospel.

They both have implemented different programs in Family/Parenting issues to help strengthen many churches nationally using their multicultural background. They are frequent speakers at Family seminars and conferences. They both serve as Elders on the Ministerial Board of their church, and premarital counselors. They are involved in their local community, where they work with the Mayor to improve their community through participation on the Park & Recreation/Library boards. They reside in Texas with their three children.

SUMMARY OF HOMESCHOOL LAWS IN THE FIFTY STATES

1. Thirty-seven states have adopted home school statutes or regulations in the following years:
   1997: DE, AK
   1996: MI
   1991: IA
   1990: NH, CT
   1989: ND, HI, ME* and OH
   1988: CO,NY, SC, NC and PA
   1987: MD, MN, VT and WV
   1986: MO
   1985: AR, FL, NM, OR, TN, WA and WY
   1984: GA, LA, RI*, and VA
   1983: WI and MT
   1982: AZ and MS
   1957: UT*
   1956: NV

(These three states still give superintendents or school boards the discretionary authority to "approve" home schools)

Note: The rules governing home schooling in Maryland, New York, and Ohio are state board of education regulations rather than statutes. The rules governing home schools in Connecticut are Department of Education "Guidelines."

2. Forty-one states **do not** require home school parents to meet any specific qualifications. The seven states which require only a high school diploma or a GED are: NC, NM, OH, PA, SC, GA, and TN (In TN, there is no qualification requirement for grades K-8 if home school is associated with a church-related school). The remaining two states have the following qualification requirements: ND requires only a high school diploma or GED, provided that the parent is monitored by a certified teacher for two years. WV allows parents with a GED or high school diploma to teach until the child reaches high school. WV parents' formal education must remain four years ahead of the student.

3. Four states...CA, KS, NY, and OH...require home school teachers to be "competent," "qualified," or "capable of teaching." In Ohio, a high school diploma or GED satisfies the qualification requirement. In California, Kansas, and New York, even less than a GED is recognized as competent. New York parents who comply with the home instruction regulation are deemed "competent."

4. At present, four states require home schools to be subject to the discretionary "approval" of the local school district, school board or state commissioner: ME, MA, RI, and UT.

5. In at least twelve states...AK, AL, CA, IL, IN, KS, KY, MI, NE, LA, PA and TX...individual home schools may operate as private or church schools. Nine of these states do not have specific home school statutes making the private school law their only realistic option under which to home school. In Ak, MI, and LA, homeschoolers have the option to operate under the private school law or home school law.

6. In five other states...CO, FL, ME, VA, and UT...groups of home schoolers, rather than individual home schools, qualify as private or church schools: In these states, home schoolers have the option to operate under either a home school law or the private school law.

7. South Carolina and Delaware are the only states in which legislature has specifically exempted **home school associations** from compulsory attendance. In South Carolina, any homeschooler enrolled in an association of 50 or more homeschoolers does not have to meet the home school law approval requirements. In Delaware, any homeschooler merely "affiliated with a home school association or organization" is exempt.

8. Oklahoma, Idaho, New Jersey, and South Dakota are the only states that do not fit into the category of a home school state, private school law state, or approval state. Oklahoma is the only state with a constitutional amendment that specifically guarantees the right to home school ("other means of education"). In Idaho, home schools simply must be "otherwise comparably instructed." No approval is involved. In New Jersey, home schools are considered under the category "elsewhere than at school." In South Dakota, they are " alternative instruction programs" along with private schools. They must annually notify and test.

9. Twenty-five states require standardized testing **or** evaluation.

   a. The following ten states require standard-ized testing <u>only</u> : AR (testing only in grades 5, 7, and 10-no other method of evaluation), GA (requires annual progress report by instructor and testing every three years), MN and NC (annual testing), NM (grades 4, 6, and 8), ND(testing only in grades 3, 4, 6, 8, and 11-no other method of evaluation), OR (grades 3, 5, 8, and 10), SD (grades 2, 4, 8, and 11), TN (5, 7, and 9), and NY (grades 9-12). (Note: MN and GA do not require submission of results to the public school);

   b. Sixteen of the 25 states provide an alterna-tive to testing: CO,CT, FL, IA, LA, HI,

ME, MA, NH, NY, OH, PA, VT, VA, WA, and WV. (CT only requires a portfolio review, and CO and WA do <u>not</u> require submission of test results or evaluation to the public school.)

10. Eight states...VA, MD, VT, NE, AL, AK, PA, TN...allow homeschoolers to obtain some type of religious exemption.

   a. **Virginia:** " A school board...shall excuse from attendance at school any pupil who, together with his parents, by reason of bona fide religious training or belief, is conscientiously opposed to attendance at school." §22. 1-257 (B)(2). No other requirements apply.

   b. **Maryland:** [P]arents may homeschool if at least fifteen days before the beginning of a home instruction program. The parent signs a notice of intent form indicating that the child's "instruction is offered through correspondence courses and is under the supervision of a school or institution offering an educational program operated by a *bona-fide church organization*."

   c. **Vermont:** "After the filing of the enrollment notice or at a hearing, if the home study program is unable to comply with any specific requirements *due to deep religious conviction* shared by an organized group. The

Commissioner may waive such requirements if he or she determines that the educational purposes of this section are being or
will be substantially met." Title 16 § 166b
(j).

d. **Nebraska:** A home school is considered a
private, denominational, or parochial school
and there must declare in writing that
"requirements for approval and accredita-
tion.....*violate sincerely held religious
beliefs* of the parents or guardians."

e. **Alabama:** Home schools qualify as church
"schools...operated as a *ministry of a local
church*, groups of churches, denomination,
and/or association of churches on a nonprofit basis which do not receive any state or
federal funding." Ala. Code § 16-28-1(2)
(emphasis added). "Every child *attending* a
church school is exempt from the requirements of this [compulsory attendance] section provided the child complies with the
procedure in § 16-28-7 [parent or guardian
reporting attendance in church school]."
Ala. Code § 16-28-3 (emphasis added).

f. **Alaska:** A home school may qualify as a
"religious or other private school" as long as
it meets the following definition: The definition of a religious school is a "private school
*operated by a church or other religious
organization* that does not receive direct

state or federal funding." Alaska Stat. § 14.45.200 (2).

g. **Tennessee:** "Home schools who teach grades K-12, whose parents are associated with an organization that *conducts church related* schools as defined by § 49-50-801…shall be exempt" from all home school requirements.

h. **Pennsylvania:** Parents may teach their children at home if the home is an extension or satellite of a religious day school. Since the law simply states a child must be "enrolled," parents may "enroll" their child in a religious day school, but teach them at home. According to § 13-1327(a), such a day school must do the following: "A child enrolled in a day school which is *operated by a bona fide church or other religious body*, and the parent, guardian or other person having control or charge of any such child or children of compulsory school age shall be deemed to have met the requirements of this section…."

11. Six states…..CT, IN, KS, ME, NJ, and NV…..require instruction or amount of time to be "equivalent" to public schools: The term "equivalent" was struck down by courts as void for vagueness in MN and MO. Three states……MD,DE, and RI…..require instruction to be "regular and thorough." One

state......ID......requires instruction to be "comparable" to public schools.

12. Higher courts in six states have ruled that their states' compulsory attendance statutes were unconstitutional because they were too vague.

   a. Georgia: the case *Roemhild* v. *State.* 308 S.E.2d 154 (Ga. 1982) resulted in Georgia's legislature passing a favorable home school law.

   b. Wisconsin: the case *State* v. *Popanz.* 332 N.W.2d 750 (Wis. 1983) also resulted in the passage of a favorable home school law.

   c. Minnesota: the case *State* v. *Newstrom.* 371 N.W.2d 525 (Minn. 1985) declared the law void because it was too vague. This resulted in the passage of a favorable home school law.

   d. Missouri: the case *Ellis* v. *O'Hara.* 612 F. Supp. 379 (E.D. Mo. 1985) declared the law void because it was too vague. This resulted in the passage of a favorable home school law. After the home school law was passed, the *Ellis* case was reversed as moot. 802 F.2d 462 (8th Cir. 1986).

   e. Iowa: *Fellowship Baptist Church* v. *Benton,* 815 F .2d 485 (8th Cir. 1987) upheld the certification requirements against private schools and remanded to a district court the issue of the vagueness of the equivalent instruction requirements. The district court ruled new administrative regulations cured the vagueness of the statute. 678 F. Supp. 213 (S.D. Iowa 1988).

f. Pennsylvania: the case *Jeffery* v. *O'Donnell*, 702 F. Supp. 516 (M.D. PA 1988) ruled that compulsory attendance was unconstitutionally vague as applied to home schools. This resulted in the passage of a favorable home school law.

STATES WHICH HAVE PASSED PARENTAL RIGHTS ACTS

1. Michigan
M.C.L.A. §380.10.

It is the natural, fundamental right of parents and legal guardians to determine and direct the care, teaching, and education of their children.

2. Kansas
K.S.A. Sec. 159

(b) Parents shall retain the fundamental right to exercise primary control over the care and upbringing of their children in their charge.

(c) Any parent may maintain a cause of action in a federal or state court, or before an administrative tribunal of appropriate jurisdiction for claims arising under 42 U.S.C. 1983 and any damages resulting therefrom or arising under the principles established in subsection (b) .

(d) Upon the finding by the court of a substantial basis for claim, the court shall award attorney fees to the parent.

3. Texas

S.B. 359 (signed into law, 1997). Mandates that the CPS "shall not contradict the fundamental rights of parents to direct the education and upbringing of their children."

H.B. 425 (also signed into law, 1997) "No state agency may adopt rules or policies or take any other action which violates the fundamental right and duty of parents to direct the upbringing of the parents' child ."

CREDIT

This appendix section was provided by Home School Legal Defense association-HSLDA. Be advised that this appendix section **does not** constitute in any way legal counsel. To purchase a comprehensive summary of the laws for all 50 states, or to receive HSLDA's membership application contact HSLDA through any of the following: HSLDA, P.O.Box 3000, Purcellvile, VA 20134. www. hslda.org or call (540) 338-5600.